FORCE PROTECTION

Air Force Doctrine Document 3-10
28 July 2011

This document complements related discussion found in Joint Publications 1, *Doctrine for the Armed Forces of the United States*; 3-07.2, *Antiterrorism*, and 3-10, *Joint Security Operations in Theater.*

BY ORDER OF THE
SECRETARY OF THE AIR FORCE

AIR FORCE DOCTRINE DOCUMENT 3-10
28 JULY 2011

SUMMARY OF CHANGES

This document has been substantially revised and should be completely reviewed. The document has been renumbered to comply with the new doctrine architecture established in Air Force Instruction 10-1301, *Air Force Doctrine*. The focus of force protection has been expanded from an agile combat support perspective to responsibilities held by commanders at all levels (Chapter 1). The discussion on the definition for force protection has been expanded to clarify the Service perspective (Chapter 1). The discussion of command responsibilities has been greatly expanded (Chapter 2). Force protection's focus in the Air Force on both threats and hazards has been expanded (Chapter 3). The force protection planning process to counter threats and hazards using the risk management process has been expanded, with the addition of a criticality assessment to the process (Chapter 4). Information describing the base security zone and its relationship to the base boundary was added (Chapter 4). A new discussion on the force protection community has been added (Chapter 5). Terminology and vignettes have been updated throughout.

Supersedes: AFDD 2-4.1, 9 Nov 04
OPR: LeMay Center/DDS
Certified by: LeMay Center/DD (Col Christian Watt)
Pages: 45
Accessibility: Available on the e-publishing website at www.e-publishing.af.mil for downloading
Releasability: There are no releasability restrictions on this publication
Approved by: DAVID S. FADOK, Major General, USAF
            Commander, LeMay Center for Doctrine Development and Education

FOREWORD

Due to the increased lethality of international and domestic threats, it is imperative the Air Force take strong measures to protect our personnel and installations, both at home and abroad. How the Air Force protects its forces is critical to global engagement. An air and space expeditionary task force poised to respond to global taskings within hours must establish the means and will to fully protect its forces.

Commanders at all levels must have an effective force protection program. Commanders are responsible for protecting their people and the warfighting resources necessary to perform any military operation. We are obligated by the moral necessity of protecting our Airmen to ensure force protection is a part of Air Force culture.

The Air Force must continue to develop and refine doctrine that promotes the most effective way to achieve force protection. Understanding and using this doctrine will help ensure the successful protection of our people and resources.

DAVID S. FADOK
Major General, USAF
Commander, LeMay Center for Doctrine
Development and Education

TABLE OF CONTENTS

PREFACE

Air Force Doctrine Document (AFDD) 3-10, *Force Protection*, is the Air Force's operational level doctrinal publication on force protection. Force protection supports the core function of Agile Combat Support, and its supporting capability of "Protect the Force."[1] Protecting Air Force personnel and resources is critical to the Service's ability to perform its mission.

Chapter 1, *Force Protection Fundamentals*, defines force protection for the Air Force and describes how the Air Force views force protection as compared to the multinational and joint views. It describes the basic features of force protection and provides a description of the military challenges faced by commanders and Airmen responsible for force protection, the unique perspective they provide, and general procedures that guide their actions.

Chapter 2, *Command Responsibilities for Force Protection*, describes command relationships when addressing force protection concerns and illustrates how Air Force forces are presented to a joint force commander as part of the commander of Air Force forces' air and space expeditionary task force. It also shows how these relationships integrate into ongoing operations conducted by other national-level US government agencies and host nation counterparts, and describes legal considerations for force protection.

Chapter 3, *Threats and Hazards to the Air Force Mission*, describes the many threats and hazards faced by Air Force personnel and identifies the various levels of threat that exist throughout the range of military operations. It further discusses Department of Defense terrorism threat levels assessed by the Defense Intelligence Agency as well as force protection conditions as used by geographic combatant commanders. It provides a discussion of threat objectives and hazard effects.

Chapter 4, *Force Protection Planning*, introduces risk management as a process to assist decision makers in reducing or offsetting risks. It gives an overview of the process; identifies the goals, key aspects, and principle concepts of the process; and provides general guidelines for applying the process. The chapter discusses force protection planning considerations, describing the direct relationship between force protection and risk management.

Chapter 5, *The Force Protection Community*, discusses the concepts of integrated defense, emergency management, the critical infrastructure program, and force protection effects.

Air Force doctrine expands and elaborates upon existing joint doctrine which does not explicitly describe the philosophical underpinnings of any one Service, nor does it describe how a Service organizes to support a joint force commander. These

---

[1] See AFDD 4-0, *Agile Combat Support.*

are Service, not joint, prerogatives. The ideas presented here should enable Airmen to better describe what the Air Force can provide to the joint effort for force protection. AFDD 3-10 should influence creation of corresponding joint and multinational doctrine, and may affect the doctrine of other Services as well.

The principal audience for this publication consists of all Airmen, military and civilian.

CHAPTER ONE

FORCE PROTECTION FUNDAMENTALS

> *...as a result of the coalition successes in DESERT SHIELD/DESERT STORM, coupled with American dominance in the skies, terrorists have focused on vulnerabilities on the ground. As a result, the Air Force can no longer consider overseas locations as risk-free sanctuaries from which to operate. The Air Force must institutionalize a completely different force protection mindset. The Air Force must inculcate this new mindset into every Service member through all levels of education and training, from accession to separation. Further, an enduring organizational structure must be established that will ensure force protection remains on course through frequent reviews which address threat dynamics.*
>
> **—Lt Gen James F. Record, USAF,**
> **Independent review of the Khobar Towers bombing,**
> **31 October 1996**

The 21st Century has, thus far, been characterized by a significant shift in Air Force responsibilities and an increased exposure of its resources to worldwide threats. This point is underscored by the terrorist attacks of 11 September 2001 and the ongoing overseas contingency operations. Today, potential opponents are more unpredictable, capable, and lethal, leveraging the increased availability of high and low technology weapons, including weapons of mass destruction (WMD). The Air Force's ability to project US airpower requires protection from these threats at home, in transit, and abroad.

FORCE PROTECTION DEFINED

The Air Force defines force protection (FP) as **"[t]he process of detecting threats and hazards to the Air Force and its mission, and applying measures to deter, pre-empt, negate or mitigate them based on an acceptable level of risk."**[2] FP is a fundamental principle of all military operations as a way to ensure the survivability of a commander's forces. The Air Force takes an integrated approach to FP in order to conserve the force's fighting potential.

Joint doctrine defines force protection as "[p]reventive measures taken to mitigate hostile actions against Department of Defense personnel (to include family members), resources, facilities, and critical information. Force protection does not

---

[2] The Air Force definition is derived from historical best practices and analysis. It is updated from the definition from AFDD 2-4.1, *Force Protection*, 9 Nov 04.

include actions to defeat the enemy or protect against accidents, weather, or disease."[3] The Air Force's integrated approach demands these key effects omitted from the joint definition be incorporated in the Air Force's approach to FP if the Air Force is to protect its forces and mission. Consequently, the Air Force includes actions to both defeat the enemy and protect against hazards such as accidents, weather, disease, and natural disasters.

A comparison of North Atlantic Treaty Organization (NATO), joint, and single Service definitions is therefore instructive; it helps frame the basis for the agreed-upon Air Force definition. NATO doctrine explains that "[t]he operational environment may have no discernable 'front-lines' or 'rear area' and an adversary may be expected to target Allied vulnerabilities anywhere with a wide range of capabilities."[4] Consequently, NATO defines FP as "[m]easures and means to minimize the vulnerability of personnel, facilities, materiel, operations, and activities from threats and hazards in order to preserve freedom of action and operational effectiveness thereby contributing to mission success."[5]

FORCE PROTECTION FUNDAMENTALS

All Airmen should know the fundamental aspects of FP to safeguard their own lives, those of fellow Airmen, and valuable Air Force resources. Key to the Air Force view of FP is the protection of its people, the prime asset of the Service. Further, all Airmen are expected to contribute to force protection as both a sensor and as a warrior, prepared to protect and defend operations and assets.

As opposed to viewing protection and security as independent processes, **the Air Force takes a more holistic approach to FP than is described in the joint definition for the term**. To this end, risk management, along with protection against natural hazards and disease, are elements of FP execution for the Air Force. Protection is defined as "[p]reservation of the effectiveness and survivability of mission-related military and nonmilitary personnel, equipment, facilities, information, and infrastructure deployed or located within or outside the boundaries of a given operational area."[6] Security is defined as "[m]easures taken by a military unit, activity, or installation to protect itself against all acts designed to, or which may, impair its effectiveness."[7] Rather than bifurcating efforts under these two related concepts, the Air Force treats FP as a whole entity for commanders to act upon.

Effective FP is more than just a law enforcement, antiterrorism (AT), or security function. Prior to the 1996 bombing of Khobar Towers in Saudi Arabia, the closest term to "force protection" used with any frequency was "antiterrorism," which

---

[3] Joint Publication (JP) 1-02, *DOD Dictionary of Military and Associated Terms*.
[4] Allied Joint Publication 3.14, *Allied Joint Doctrine for Force Protection*.
[5] Ibid.
[6] JP 1-02.
[7] Ibid.

was often viewed as a law enforcement-only function with some focus on individual protective measures.[8] FP now receives greater attention and is more integrated and cross-functional. It has also been routinely confused as being synonymous with antiterrorism, hence the erroneous term "AT/FP." This use of AT and FP in this manner has led to a mindset that AT and FP are synonymous. FP is actually much broader in scope, serving as the overarching ends integrating all relevant programs and efforts. Security Forces, augmentees, and owner/user personnel (e.g., personnel working in maintenance and operations on and around a flightline) provide security. Intelligence and counterintelligence personnel provide as accurate a threat picture as possible, and shape decision-making with intelligence preparation of the operational environment products. Civil engineers design physical security improvements, provide emergency management planning, training, and response capabilities to deal with force protection-related events, and provide explosive ordnance disposal capabilities; medical and emergency management personnel conduct presumptive identification for the presence of biological or chemical agents; and communications specialists integrate evacuation

Khobar Towers

It doesn't matter who they are. Everybody's a sensor now. There aren't enough cops out there to see everything. It's everybody's responsibility to report what's going on.

—Staff Sergeant Alfredo Guerrero, the first to see the gas truck that destroyed Khobar Towers on 25 June 1996, at Dhahran Air Base, Saudi Arabia.

notification systems.[9] These are only examples of the breadth of FP in the Air Force.

Every Airman is a sensor, and protecting the force is everyone's duty.[10] All Airmen are responsible for FP, whether reporting suspicious activity while engaged in their primary duties, augmenting base defense, or assisting in response to a natural disaster. This responsibility can stress available personnel and resources. In the end, commanders should balance mission accomplishment with FP and embrace the "every Airman is a warrior" culture, enlisting the whole force in protecting or defending an air base. All military Airmen should be trained and equipped to protect and defend the base against all threats and hazards, and commanders should be identified to lead them in the effort. This includes basic ground combat skills training (e.g., weapons familiarization, self-aid/buddy care), disaster response procedures, and other relevant training required to prepare Airmen to better protect themselves and the base. Additionally, all Airmen should be trained to recognize and report chemical, biological,

---

[8] DOD Directive 2000.12, *DOD Antiterrorism Program.*
[9] AFDD 4-0, *Combat Support.*
[10] Quotation by James G. Roche, Secretary of the Air Force, 2001-05.

radiological, nuclear, and high-yield explosive (CBRNE) hazards, which can be difficult to detect and may not always be preceded by a recognizable hostile event.

FP is multi-dimensional, providing multi-layered protection of forces and resources. It covers actions at home station, in transit, and at deployed locations. It includes not only protecting military members and civilian employees, but also their families, contract employees, and visitors while on an installation.[11] In addition, a broad array of integrated functional expertise is necessary to facilitate a seamless FP posture. This functional expertise includes intelligence collection; awareness and reporting by all Airmen, on and off duty; detection of and protection from CBRN hazards, along with high yield explosives; physical security enhancements; armed defense; law enforcement liaison; and numerous other areas of expertise.[12] This multi-layered protection extends awareness and influence as far forward as possible, while simultaneously providing in-depth protection to Air Force personnel and resources. This maximizes the ability to disrupt attacks and provide the earliest warning possible, while ensuring the best protection for the Service's most valuable assets, its people, through close-in security. The end result is Air Force forces able to conduct their missions with the best protection available, based on risk management, wherever the mission is.

FP requires a global orientation because of the Air Force's worldwide presence and its ability to move quickly across great distances in the pursuit of theater and national objectives. Deploying personnel and those traveling for other reasons should focus on their changing environments. For example, they should be aware of the assessed threat and hazards at their home station and at each location they will transit, examine the vulnerabilities associated with their travel, and develop a personal protection plan.

Effective intelligence, surveillance, and reconnaissance (ISR); counterintelligence; and liaison efforts are critical to identifying, analyzing, and disseminating threat and hazard information to commanders and ensuring force protection. Threats may include conventional military units, special forces, foreign intelligence agents and services, terrorist groups, aggressive civil populations, criminal elements, extremist groups, or insider threats operating in, through, and across multiple domains. The enemy may use weapons such as improvised explosive devices (IEDs) or vehicle borne IEDs (VBIEDs), mortars, rockets, man-portable air defense systems, computer viruses, CBRN material and agents, and high yield explosives. Hazards may include hazardous waste, unstable infrastructure, inclement weather, disease vectors, unfamiliar culture, and other factors. Tactics may include conventional as well as asymmetrical methods. Commanders should develop critical information requirements to guide force protection intelligence (FPI) work supporting their decision-making and operations. FPI is analyzed, all-source intelligence information that, when integrated or fused with other FP information, provides an assessment of the threats to DOD missions, people, or resources. FPI is proactive and drives FP decisions in support of

---

[11] JP 1, *Doctrine for the Armed Forces of the United States*, establishes the responsibilities of geographic combatant commanders for force protection. See Chapter 2 for a more detailed discussion of command relationships as they affect FP.
[12] See AFDD 3-40, *Counter-Chemical, Biological, Radiological, and Nuclear Operations.*

commander's intent.[13] Personnel at all levels should coordinate with cross-functional counterparts (e.g., Intelligence, Air Force Office of Special Investigations [AFOSI], Security Forces, AT officers, installation emergency managers, weather, etc., as well as the counterparts to these entities in other Services in theater and local or host nation forces) to share information and ensure FPI requirements are satisfied in accordance with DOD and Air Force guidance. Constant liaison with local counterparts and host nation forces also enhances cooperation and willingness to share information, especially in crisis situations. Figure 1.1 portrays an information sharing strategy used in the ISR community, illustrating the importance of this cooperation necessary for intelligence to support FP.

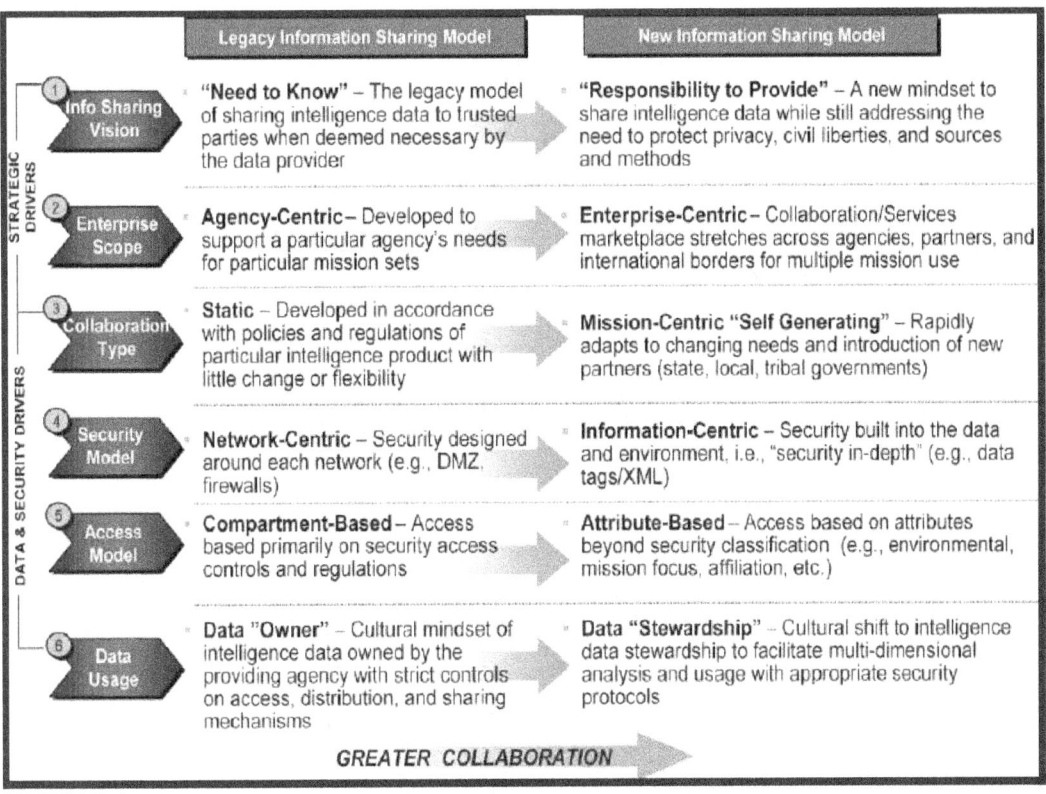

Figure 1.1. United States Intelligence Community Information Sharing Strategy, 22 Feb 08, (Office of the Director of National Intelligence)

FP practitioners use new technology to enhance capabilities. Technology offers force protectors advantages in speed, range, and effectiveness to assist them in meeting the demands of a changing operational environment. For example, use of small, remotely piloted aircraft extends tactical situational awareness for base defense. However, none of these technologies can perform FP alone. As technology evolves, so do the tactics of adversaries, necessitating changes in the response to threats. FP

---

[13] Definition derived from AFI 14-119, *Intelligence Support to Force Protection*. See Air Force Tactics, Techniques, and Procedures (AFTTP) 3-10.2, *Integrated Base Defense Command and Control*, for additional information.

requires continued vigilance by the members of the force being protected, with technology acting to enhance their capabilities, not to replace them.

FP is both an individual and a command responsibility. Individuals should know the assessed threat against them and their vulnerabilities at their current location, along their route of travel, and at their destination. They should also know and implement individual protective measures. In addition, individuals should immediately report suspicious activities or occurrences to the nearest Security Forces, AFOSI, or local law enforcement officer. Immediate reporting increases the chance that information collected is analyzed and turned into intelligence to support the commander.

THE AIRMAN'S PERSPECTIVE

"Airminded" Force Protection. Airmen normally think of airpower and the application of force from a functional rather than geographical perspective. Airmen do not divide up the battlefield into areas of operation as do surface forces.[14] Airmen typically approach battle in terms of the effects they create on the adversary, rather than on the nature and location of specific targets.[15] This approach normally leads to more inclusive and comprehensive perspectives that favor strategic solutions over tactical ones. This perspective extends to the Service's views on force protection. Unlike surface forces that differentiate between security and protection, the Air Force's holistic approach is better suited to accomplishing its missions.

How Air Force forces are commanded and organized to execute force protection responsibilities is influenced by this Airman's perspective. Because of the unique strategic nature of air, space and cyberspace operations, Airmen have developed a distinct perspective that guides how they think about their operational warfighting domains. General Henry "Hap" Arnold referred to this *Airman's perspective* as "airmindedness."[16] This airmindedness reflects the range, speed, and capabilities of air, space, and cyberspace forces, as well as threats and survival imperatives unique to Airmen. Airmen have a common understanding of air, space, and cyberspace operations, the threats and hazards to those operations, and the role they play in defending them. The Airman's perspective is an approach that shapes the conduct of operations and training to maximize operational effectiveness. It is built and developed through shared culture, ethos, values, and experience and makes a major contribution to an agile, flexible, expeditionary Air Force able to protect its force regardless of place or circumstance. Airmen should use their Airmen's perspective to drive how FP is applied in support of air, space, and cyberspace operations.

---

[14] Col Dennis M. Drew, *Joint Operations: The World Looks Different from 10,000 Feet* (*Airpower Journal*, Fall 1988), http://www.airpower.maxwell.af.mil/airchronicles/apj/apj88/fal88/drew.html, accessed 6 Jan 09. For additional information on the Airman's Perspective, see AFDD 1, *Air Force Basic Doctrine, Organization, and Command.*

[15] Air Force Doctrine Document (AFDD) 1, pp. 19-ff; AFDD 3-60, *Targeting*, pp. 1-2.

[16] Gen Henry H. "Hap" Arnold, *Third Report of the Commanding General of the Army Air Forces to the Secretary of War* (Baltimore, Md: Schneidereith, 12 November 1945), 70.

CHAPTER TWO

COMMAND RESPONSIBILITIES FOR FORCE PROTECTION

> *Defense of air bases against ground attack has been traditionally viewed within the USAF as a Security Police [sic] problem. We judge that it is more properly viewed as an **airpower** problem because airpower is so critical to US national military strategy and the US way of war. This criticalness makes air base defense ultimately a **joint** problem.*
>
> **—David Shlapak and Alan Vick,**
> ***Check Six Begins on the Ground:***
> ***Responding to the Evolving Ground Threat to US Air Force Bases***

Centralized control and decentralized execution of force protection measures and resources are essential to protect forces against threats and hazards worldwide. Force protection is a task for every commander at every level. Clarity of command responsibilities for FP is essential for a comprehensive, unambiguous, and integrated response. Integration of all aspects of FP, including interoperability with civilian command and control systems, should enable commanders to react quickly to threats and hazards. The legal basis for commanders' force protection authority has been greatly clarified in recent years, and it is essential that commanders understand their responsibilities and jurisdictions. Discussion of FP command responsibilities begins above the Air Force organizations in a joint force because of the top-down guidance that permeates the military in support of FP.

THE ROLE OF THE GEOGRAPHIC COMBATANT COMMANDER

Force protection is not exclusively a Service responsibility. According to both the Unified Command Plan and Joint Publication (JP) 1, *Doctrine for the Armed Forces of the United States,* **geographic combatant commanders (GCC) have the overall requirement to establish and implement FP in their areas of responsibility (AORs).** GCCs exercise authority for force protection over all DOD personnel (including their dependents) assigned, attached, transiting through, or training in the GCC's AOR, except for those for whom the Department of State Chief of Mission retains security responsibility.[17]

Tactical Control Authority for Force Protection

Inherent in a GCC's authority is the power to lawfully delegate specific command authority to subordinate commanders, such as a commander of Air Force forces (COMAFFOR), to accomplish missions. For instance, as authority for FP flows from the

---

[17] JP 1, *Doctrine for the Armed Forces of the United States*, Chapter 1, para 5.d.2.; Chapter 4, para 2.c.; Chapter 5, para 1.b.(1).(d).; and Chapter 5, para 2.f.

GCC, it is normally delegated as a tactical control (TACON) authority to subordinate commanders at any echelon at or below the level of combatant commander.[18] TACON for FP is recognized as a specified form of TACON, and is used by subordinate commanders as the command relationship over all personnel assigned, attached, or in transit for the explicit purpose of FP, regardless of Service. This exercise of TACON for FP is an exception to the normal limitation of commanders in an AOR exercising chain of command authority over transient forces. This force protection authority ensures unity of command and enables subordinate commanders, under the auspices of exercising TACON for FP in support of the GCC, the ability to change, modify, prescribe and enforce force protection measures for affected forces.

Although geographic combatant commanders may delegate authority to accomplish the FP mission, they may not absolve themselves of the responsibility for the attainment of those missions. Authority is never absolute; the extent of authority is specified by the establishing authority, directives, and law.

Force Protection in US Northern Command

In most theaters, the senior DOD member serves as the combatant commander and assumes FP responsibilities. In US Northern Command's (USNORTHCOM's) AOR, where the Secretary of Defense and other senior DOD officials outrank the USNORTHCOM commander, the combatant commander maintains responsibility for FP. While this is a unique situation for USNORTHCOM, the principle is the same–there must be a commander responsible for the protection of DOD assets in the USNORTHCOM AOR to ensure unity of effort, and that commander is the commander, USNORTHCOM. The Title 10, United States Code, requirements of the military departments to support USNORTHCOM are the same as in any other theater, including supporting the USNORTHCOM FP mission.

USNORTHCOM executes a comprehensive all-hazards approach to provide an appropriate level of safety and security for the DOD elements (to include the Reserve components, DOD civilians, family members, and contractors supporting DOD at DOD facilities or installations), resources, infrastructure, information, and equipment from the threat spectrum to assure mission success.[19] The authorities of commanders in the USNORTHCOM AOR are similar to those of commanders in other geographic combatant command AORs.

---

[18] CJCSM 3150.13C, 10 March 2010, Joint Reporting Structure – Personnel Manual.
[19] USNORTHCOM Instruction 10-222, *USNORTHCOM Force Protection Mission and Antiterrorism Program.*

FORCE PROTECTION AND COMMAND RELATIONSHIPS IN A JOINT ENVIRONMENT

The Joint Force Commander

Since protecting the force is an overarching mission responsibility inherent in the command of all military operations, joint force commanders (JFCs) should consider FP in the same fashion that they consider other aspects of military operations, such as movement and maneuver; intelligence, surveillance, and reconnaissance; employing firepower; sustaining operations in a CBRNE environment; and providing command and control during the execution of operations across the range of military operations (ROMO). The GCC or a subordinate joint task force (JTF) commander can delineate the force protection measures for all DOD personnel not under the responsibility of the Department of State. If a JFC designates command of an installation to a specific Service component commander, that commander has TACON for FP over all personnel on that installation, regardless of Service or status. For instance, if an Air Force commander is given FP responsibility for an installation, it is his or her responsibility to coordinate FP operations with commanders in adjoining or surrounding geographic regions; this includes intelligence sharing and deconfliction of operations that span the seams between operational areas.

The Service authority of administrative control (ADCON) is used to support various measures of FP, but is not the appropriate term to describe where the responsibility for implementation lies. For example, each Service may have ADCON responsibility to equip its personnel deploying to a hostile environment with appropriate body armor, but the requirement to wear that armor, and under what circumstances, is the responsibility of the commander on the ground at the deployed location, as these are operational, not administrative, decisions. As the JFC normally delegates operational control (OPCON) to the COMAFFOR for all Air Force forces assigned or attached, the COMAFFOR normally exercises TACON for FP over those forces. TACON for FP over Air Force forces also resides with the joint commander of another Service who has Air Force forces attached with specification of TACON for a given responsibility.

Commander, Air Force Forces

In any operation in which the Air Force presents forces to a JFC, there will be a designated COMAFFOR who serves as the commander of US Air Force forces assigned or attached to the US Air Force component. The COMAFFOR, with the air expeditionary task force, presents the JFC a task-organized, integrated package with the proper balance of force sustainment and force protection elements. This applies on installations when the JFC has designated an Air Force officer as the base commander, i.e., when the Air Force is the primary occupant of a base.[20]

---

[20] JP 3-10, Chapter II, para 3.b.(8).

Commanders at appropriate subordinate echelons (such as wing, group, and squadron level) retain ultimate responsibility for protecting persons and property subject to their control and have the authority to enforce security measures. To this end, those commanders should ensure FP standards are met and make it an imperative to have an effective force protection program. These commanders face three major FP challenges: planning for FP integration and support as tasked in applicable operational plans, training for FP, and providing FP for those interests within their influence. These commanders have the added responsibility of accomplishing FP planning for the units identified to deploy to their location during contingency operations. Commanders should designate a member of their staffs as the integrator of FP subject matter experts to establish guidance for, program for, and manage FP requirements for their organizations. Figure 2.1 illustrates a notional COMAFFOR staff with the FP officer location identified.

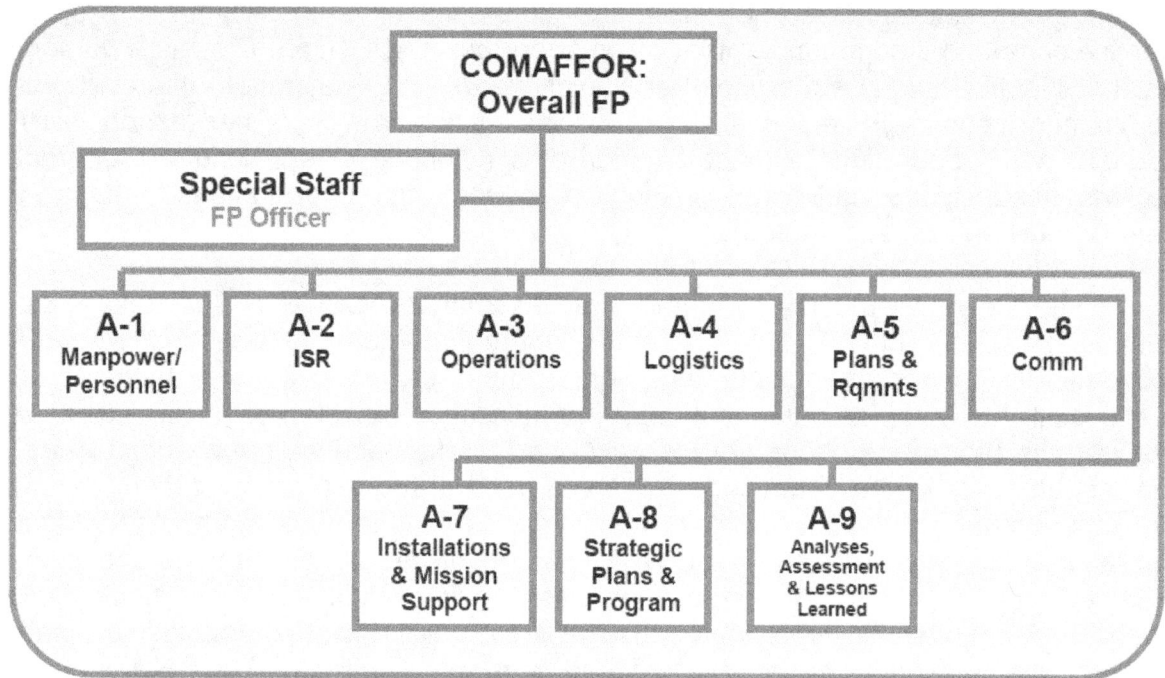

Figure 2.1. COMAFFOR Staff with FP officer location identified.
Note: This individual is normally titled the "AT officer," a term defined in DODI 2000.16 and used in Joint Publication 3-07.2, *Antiterrorism*, to describe that person responsible to a commander for force protection planning and advisory responsibilities.

LEGAL AND LAW ENFORCEMENT CONSIDERATIONS DURING FP PLANNING AND EXECUTION

Force protection fundamentals are applied in many different operational environments and organization command structures. In the course of planning, commanders should maintain an awareness of legal constraints that may affect operations. Information relevant to the use of force is contained in international law, US law, host nation law, the law of armed conflict, and established rules of engagement or rules for the use of force. Together, these laws and rules regulate the status and activities of forces across the ROMO. Below are some legal requirements a commander should consider, depending on where force protection measures are being implemented.

Types of Jurisdiction

Depending upon where an incident occurs on an installation or within the base boundary, jurisdiction may differ as it is rare for an installation to have just one type of jurisdiction throughout. For instances involving areas under government control where the Air Force does not exercise exclusive federal jurisdiction, commanders should work closely with the staff judge advocate and relevant authorities to establish protocols for handling civilian violators. When an installation is located within a foreign nation, jurisdiction may be governed by the terms of a status of forces agreement or other agreement with the particular host nation. Likewise, in these areas where authority and jurisdiction constraints prevent organic security forces from patrolling or otherwise occupying areas outside the installation's recognized base boundary but within the base security zone (BSZ), commanders should apply risk management to minimize risk exposure to assets and personnel. They should also coordinate security requirements with local authorities and adjacent friendly forces. For additional information on the BSZ and base boundary, see Chapter 4.

Legal considerations for Homeland Operations

In the US, commanders publish and enforce regulations to protect installation resources and force protection intelligence[21] is vital to painting an accurate picture for a commander to better anticipate and plan against threats and hazards. However, due diligence should be given to intelligence oversight issues when carrying out the FPI process. The duties and obligations placed on DOD intelligence organizations to protect the rights of individuals stem from the U.S. Constitution, Presidential Executive Order 12333, and DOD Regulation 5240.1-R, *Procedures Governing the Activities of DOD Intelligence Components that Affect United States Persons*, which spells out how the Presidential Executive Order applies to Defense intelligence activities. In a similar manner, DOD members not part of the intelligence community have obligations stemming from the U.S. Constitution, Title 5 of the United States Code (the "Privacy Act"), and DOD Directive 5200.27, *Acquisition of Information Concerning Persons and Organizations not Affiliated with the Department of Defense*. Specific Air Force guidance is contained in AFI 14-104, *Oversight of Intelligence Activities*.[22] The primary objective of a commander's intelligence oversight program is to ensure units and staff organizations conducting intelligence activities do not infringe on or violate the rights of US persons. Commanders should implement safeguards to ensure the conduct of force protection activities conform to US law, executive orders, and DOD directives. These tools ensure that FP operations do not violate intelligence oversight directives.

---

[21] For additional information on FPI, see Chapter 4.

[22] Staff organizations and non-intelligence organizations can perform intelligence-related activities that can collect, analyze, process, retain, or disseminate information on US persons and those who exercise command over these units and organizations. For additional information, see AFI 14-104, Chapter 3.

Likewise, commanders should understand the degree of control they have over their installations, and be familiar with the concepts of title and jurisdiction.[23]

INTELLIGENCE OVERSIGHT RELATED TO CONTINENTAL UNITED STATES (CONUS) FORCE PROTECTION

Intelligence oversight involves a balancing of two fundamental interests: obtaining the intelligence information required to protect national security and protecting individual rights guaranteed by the Constitution and the laws of the United States. DOD 5240.1-R and AFI 14-104, *Oversight of Intelligence Activities*, provide the standards for intelligence oversight. Air Force intelligence components should focus on threats to DOD personnel, installations, and activities posed by foreign intelligence or international terrorist entities, or those domestic groups specifically identified by the DOD Director of Counterintelligence as posing a threat to the DOD. If, during the course of routine activities and authorized missions, Air Force intelligence components receive information identifying US persons alleged to threaten DOD personnel, installations or activities, that information should be passed to the threatened DOD organization and the entity that has responsibility for countering the threat.

—Various Sources

---

[23] For a more detailed discussion of the types of jurisdiction in the homeland, see *The Military Commander and the Law*, available at http://milcom.jag.af.mil/. Sources for the DOD intelligence oversight program and the types of jurisdiction come from multiple sources: Executive Order 12333, DOD Regulation 5240.1-R; U.S. Constitution, art. I, §8, cl. 17; U.S. Constitution, art. VI, cl.2; 40 U.S.C. §§3111 and 3112; Greer v. Spock, 424 U.S. 828 (1976); and AFI 32-9001, Acquisition of Real Property (27 July 1994).

CHAPTER THREE

THREATS AND HAZARDS TO THE AIR FORCE MISSION

> *It is easier and more effective to destroy the enemy's aerial power by destroying his nests and eggs on the ground than to hunt his flying birds in the air.*
>
> **—Giulio Douhet**

The threats and hazards facing the Air Force are broad and extensive. They range from powerful state actors with the full range of conventional and CBRN weapons delivered by sophisticated means or dangerous and ingenious non-state actors with inventive and asymmetric methods of delivering scalable harm to our forces to natural disasters such as hurricanes, tornadoes, and wildfires. Such threats and hazards can create an unpredictable environment capable of inflicting apocalyptic damage with or without notice. Consequently, Air Force personnel, aircraft, equipment, installations, operating locations, and, by extension, the Air Force mission are vulnerable to a wide variety of threats and hazards. This potentially daunting paradigm demands FP awareness and education at all levels and effective FP measures that are implemented through a coherent and coordinated FP command structure.

FORCE PROTECTION THREAT AND HAZARD SPECTRUM

It is the commander's responsibility to recognize threats and hazards to the Air Force and its mission across the continuum of operations from peacetime through wartime and therefore consider the intentional objectives of threat actors or unintentional effects of hazards. There are a variety of threats and hazards facing the Air Force. Threats and hazards may arise from terrorists or insurgents, insiders, criminal entities, foreign intelligence and security services (FISS), opposing military forces, activist organizations, and natural or manmade disasters, major accidents, or medical incidents.

Prior to the attack on Khobar Towers in June 1996, the largest terrorist strike occurred in Riyadh in November 1995 at the Office of Program Management-Saudi Arabian National Guard (OPM-SANG). In this occurrence, terrorists detonated 220 pounds of TNT which resulted in 5 American deaths and 30 injuries. US officials assumed terrorists in Saudi Arabia would be unable to assemble conventional explosives of greater power than that used in the Riyadh attack, and consequently force protection measures then corresponded to the anticipated threat. The vulnerability assessment conducted for the 4404th Wing (Provisional), which included Khobar Towers, focused on five scenarios, never considering the magnitude of explosive power that would be employed there.[24] In the Khobar Towers attack, a truck laden with 20,000 pounds of TNT was detonated, destroying the building and killing 19 Americans. In

1995	1996	2003
OPM-SANG	Khobar Towers	Riyadh
Bombing	Bombing	compound
		bombing

another scenario in 2003, three housing complexes were simultaneously attacked in Riyadh. In this case, trucks loaded with explosives were driven behind vehicles designed to penetrate the compound defenses. In each case, the attackers appear to have placed little priority on their own survival.

On 29 August 2005, Keesler Air Force Base sustained a direct hit from Hurricane Katrina, at the time a Category 3 level storm. Although the base had evacuated nonessential personnel and aircraft in advance, the base's industrial and housing areas sustained damage. The storm surge covered half the base with flood water, in some places over six feet. By 31 August, relief flights were landing at the base, evacuating the first group of Airmen on 1 September.

The above events demonstrate that, in addition to addressing the threats and hazards below, Airmen should continually think "outside the box" and conduct "what if" scenarios to counter potential future threats and hazards that have not yet been planned for or seen. Tactics and procedures introduced in one theater could be seen again in other regions and may result in increased FP measures due to the threat of attack or risk of hazards which could affect ongoing operations.

Types of Threats and Hazards

In addition to those threats known to exist, there is the paradox of attempting to counter threats or hazards currently not known to exist. The types of threats and hazards listed below provide general categories; this list is not exhaustive, but can be used as a guide.

⊙ **Conventional Threat**—Regular military forces supported by a recognized government are categorized as a conventional threat. Included in this threat are tactical air, land, and sea forces.

⊙ **Unconventional Threat**—This threat encompasses a broad spectrum of military and paramilitary operations predominantly conducted through, with, or by indigenous or surrogate forces who are organized, trained, equipped, supported, and directed in varying degrees by an external source. It includes guerrilla warfare and other direct

---

[24] Information derived from the findings published in the unclassified Independent Review of the Khobar Towers Bombing, led by Lieutenant General James F. Record, 31 Oct 96.

offensive, low visibility, covert, or clandestine operations, as well as the indirect activities of subversion, sabotage, intelligence activities, and evasion and escape networks.

○ **Terrorism Threat**—This threat involves the calculated use of violence or threat of violence to instill fear and is intended to coerce or intimidate governments or societies in the pursuit of goals that are generally political, religious, or ideological. Acts of terrorism are often planned to attract widespread publicity and are designed to focus attention on the existence, cause, or demands of the terrorists, and erode public confidence in the ability of a government to protect and govern the people.[25]

○ **Criminal Threat**—Criminal activity may help predict future actions or provide advanced indications and warnings of attack. For example, theft of vehicles, military identification cards, passports, or installation entry passes are potential indicators of pending hostile action. Synthesized analysis of law enforcement and counterintelligence information is necessary to identify indicators of future attacks. Aggressive and continuous liaison efforts are needed for timely information sharing and willing cooperation from host forces.

○ **Insider Threat**—This threat comes from assigned or attached personnel (military or civilian), host-country nationals (military or civilian), third country nationals (contract employees) or other persons assigned to or transiting an AOR. Any of these groups of people may threaten Air Force interests by disclosing sensitive or classified information, by making decisions that favor dissident groups, or by irregular attack. They may target individuals, groups, facilities, weapon systems, or information systems. Host country forces may not provide the degree of FP anticipated or agreed to under treaty or coalition arrangements.

○ **Psychological Threat**—Enemy threats target the psychological and physical well being of Air Force personnel. The threat of CBRNE attacks can hinder effective military operations as much as an actual attack. The enemy may also use deception (such as releasing harmless powder) to undermine the mission. Enemy propaganda and potentially biased media sources may also undermine coalition and public support, create civil unrest, and dangerously weaken military morale. Commanders should recognize the importance of effective communication to minimize FP risks.

○ **Chemical, Biological, Radiological, Nuclear, and High-yield Explosive Threats and Hazards**—The CBRNE threats and hazards are those chemical, biological, radiological, nuclear, and high-yield explosive elements that pose or could pose a hazard to individuals. These threats and hazards include those created from accidental releases, toxic industrial materials (especially air and water poisons), biological pathogens, radioactive matter, and high-yield explosives. Also included are any hazards resulting from the deliberate employment of weapons of mass destruction during military operations.

---

[25] For additional information, see JP 3-07.2, *Antiterrorism*.

- ✪ **Civil Unrest Threat**—This threat reflects country-specific concerns of violence by the population related to friendly force operations. The threat can manifest itself during protests, demonstrations, refugee/humanitarian operations, or any other local tensions that may escalate into a direct threat to US forces. Activist groups may take active part in intentional, direct, and often militant actions to achieve economic, environmental, political, or social change in hopes of imposing their ideologies.

- ✪ **Information/Data Threat**—This threat results from attempts to adversely affect Air Force information systems, information-based processes, and computer-based networks. The enemy and its unconventional supporters may attempt to impact military command, control, communications, and computers; disrupt support activities such as local, military, and civil financial institutions; and interfere with supervisory control and data acquisition systems used to control critical infrastructures.

- ✪ **Environmental Hazard**—Air Force assets may be threatened by hazardous waste, unstable infrastructure, inclement weather, disease vectors, unfamiliar culture, and other factors. If ignored, these threats may have serious consequences on mission accomplishment and an Airman's individual ability to support the mission.

Levels of Threat

Enemy threats to air bases and Air Force assets take many forms and include any combination of types of threat. There are three levels of threat, depicted in Figure 3.1 and defined in JP 3-10, *Joint Security Operations in Theater*, which require security responses to counter them. These threat levels aid in performing risk assessments as well as conducting force protection planning. Each level or any combination of levels may exist in an operational area either independently or simultaneously. Emphasis on specific base or lines of communication security measures may depend on the anticipated level of threat supported by intelligence. This does not imply that threat activities will occur in a specific sequence or that there is a necessary interrelationship among the levels.

Threat Levels	Examples
Level I	Agents, saboteurs, sympathizers, terrorists, civil disturbances
Level II	Small tactical units, unconventional warfare forces, guerrillas, may include significant stand-off weapons threats
Level III	Large tactical force operations, including airborne, heliborne, amphibious, infiltration, and major air operations

Figure 3.1. Threat Levels

Level I Threats. Typical Level I threats include enemy agents and terrorists whose primary missions include espionage, sabotage, and subversion. Enemy activity and individual attacks may include random or directed killing of military and civilian personnel, kidnapping, and guiding special-purpose individuals or teams to targets.

Level I threat tactics may also include hijacking air, land, and sea vehicles for use in direct attacks; the use of IEDs; random sniping; VBIEDs; surface to air missile (SAM) attacks; or individual grenade and rocket propelled grenade attacks. Civilians sympathetic to the enemy may become significant threats to US and multinational operations. They may be the most difficult to counter because they are normally not part of an established enemy agent network and their actions may be random and unpredictable. Countering criminal activities and civil disturbance requires doctrine and guidelines that differ from those used to counter conventional forces, and normally requires detailed coordination with external agencies. More significantly, based on political, cultural, or other perspectives, activities that disrupt friendly operations may be perceived as legitimate by a large number of the local populace. Countering Level I threats is a part of the day-to-day FP measures implemented by all commanders. Key to countering these threats is the active support of some portion of the civilian population, normally those sympathetic to US or multinational goals.

Level II Threats. Level II threats include small scale (considered to be less than company-sized equivalents, generally 75-200 personnel) forces conducting unconventional warfare that can pose serious threats to military forces and civilians. These attacks can cause significant disruptions to military operations as well as to the orderly conduct of local governments and services. These forces are capable of conducting well coordinated, but small scale, hit and run attacks, IED and VBIED attacks, and ambushes, and may include significant standoff weapons threats such as mortars, rockets, rocket propelled grenades, and SAMs.

Level II threats may include special operations forces that are highly trained in unconventional warfare. These activities may also include operations typically associated with attacks outlined in the Level I threat including air, land, and sea vehicle hijacking. These forces establish and activate espionage networks, collect intelligence, carry out specific sabotage missions, develop target lists, and conduct damage assessments of targets struck. They are capable of conducting raids and ambushes.

Level III Threats. Level III threats may be encountered when an enemy has the capability to project combat power by air, land, or sea anywhere into the operational area. Specific examples include airborne, heliborne, and amphibious operations; large combined arms ground force operations; and infiltration operations involving large numbers of individuals or small groups infiltrated into the operational area and committed against friendly targets. Air and missile threats to bases, base clusters,[26] lines of communication, and civilian targets may also pose risks to joint forces, presenting themselves with little warning time.

---

[26] For information on base cluster defense operations, see JP 3-10.

Level III threats necessitate a decision to commit a tactical combat force or other significant available forces to counter the threat. This threat level is normally beyond the capability of base and base cluster defense and response forces.

DOD TERRORISM THREAT LEVELS

The Department of Defense uses a standardized set of terms to describe the terrorism threat level in each country. These terms are low, moderate, significant, and high. The Defense Intelligence Agency (DIA) sets the terrorism threat level for each country based on analysis of all available information. The levels are defined by the DIA as follows:

LOW: No group is detected or the group activity is non-threatening.

MODERATE: Terrorists are present, but there are no indications of anti-US activity. The operating environment favors the host nation and the US.

SIGNIFICANT: Anti-US terrorists are present and attack personnel as their preferred method of operation or a group uses large casualty-producing attacks as its preferred method, but has limited operational activity. The operating environment is neutral.

HIGH: Anti-US terrorists are operationally active and use large casualty-producing attacks as their preferred method of operation. There is a substantial DOD presence and the operating environment favors the terrorist.

Commanders at all levels should use the DIA terrorism threat level plus their own localized FPI threat analyses as a basis for developing plans and programs to protect Service members, civilian employees, family members, facilities, and equipment within their operational areas. Force protection conditions (FPCONs)[27] are sets of specific security measures promulgated by the commander after considering a variety of factors including the threat level, current events that might increase the risk, observed suspicious activities, etc.

There is a graduated series of FPCONs ranging from baseline security measures to FPCON Delta. There is a process by which commanders at all levels can raise or lower the FPCONs based on local conditions, specific threat information, or guidance from higher headquarters. The FPCONs are:

○ Baseline Security Measures—This condition applies when a general global threat of possible terrorist activity exists and warrants a routine security posture. At a minimum, access control will be conducted at all DOD installations and facilities.

---

[27] See DOD Instruction 2000.16, *DOD Antiterrorism Standards*, and AFI 31-101, *Integrated Defense*, for a more detailed discussion and listings of FPCONs and their measures.

- FPCON Alpha—This condition applies when there is a general threat of possible terrorist activity against personnel and facilities, the nature and extent of which are unpredictable, and circumstances do not justify full implementation of FPCON Bravo measures. The measures in this force protection condition must be capable of being maintained indefinitely.

- FPCON Bravo—This condition applies when an increased and more predictable threat of terrorist activity exists. The measures in this FPCON must be capable of being maintained for weeks without causing undue hardship, affecting operational capability, and aggravating relations with local authorities.

- FPCON Charlie—This condition applies when an incident occurs or intelligence is received indicating some form of terrorist action against personnel and facilities is imminent. Implementation of measures in this FPCON for more than a short period probably will create hardship and affect the peacetime activities of the unit and its personnel.

- FPCON Delta—This condition applies in the immediate area where a terrorist attack has occurred or when intelligence has been received that terrorist action against a specific location or person is likely. Normally, this FPCON is declared as a localized condition.

THREAT OBJECTIVES AND HAZARD EFFECTS

For Airmen to fully understand the threats and hazards previously discussed, it is important to discuss possible intended threat objectives and unintended hazard effects.

Threat Objectives

Threat incidents over the years show a trend toward ever-increasing numbers of attacks and sophistication in methods. Terrorism makes up the most prominent type of threat. Terrorism methods include threats, bombing, kidnapping, hostage taking, hijacking, assassination, sabotage, arson, armed raids or attacks, and other measures to disrupt daily activities. Such actions occur rather routinely in some parts of the world, and almost anyone is a potential victim.[28] The attempted bombing on Christmas day 2009 of an airliner en route to Detroit and the bombing attempt in May 2010 in Times Square in New York have shown that these attacks can occur within the United States as well. DOD installations remain desired targets for terrorist organizations, as demonstrated by plots against locations such as the Los Angeles National Guard base in August 2005, Fort Dix in May 2007, and Stewart Air National Guard base in May 2009.

---

[28]Information derived from terrorist information located at:
http://www.dm.usda.gov/ocpm/Security%20Guide/T5terror/Intro.htm.

The persistence of threats reflects the number and intensity of conflicts around the world and the inherent difficulties of facing, assessing, and overcoming the threat objectives. There are multiple methods of attack with threat objectives designed to cause one or more of the following harmful results:

✪ Injure or kill personnel to create a tactical, operational, or strategic event.

✪ Destroy warfighting or war-supporting capabilities.

✪ Deny use of warfighting or war-supporting capabilities through damage or contamination.

✪ Deny or disrupt military operations through the threat of attack.

✪ Influence public opinion or governmental policies to comply with competing ideologies.

✪ Force nations deployed on foreign soil to end operations and depart the deployed location.

✪ Thrust a nation into civil unrest resulting in civil war.

✪ Force a government agency or corporation to alter its policies.

✪ Reduce military advantage through theft, destruction, or fraud involving military information or technology.

✪ Increase criminal activity such as kidnapping, robbery, and extortion likely to be used to finance enemy operations.

✪ Isolate and exploit real or perceived weaknesses to demonstrate a group's capability and reduce US credibility.

✪ Bring favorable attention to a terrorist organization and serve as a recruiting tool.

All Airmen involved in FP benefit from a thorough understanding of these types of threat objectives. This understanding enhances planning to counter FP threats, thereby improving the FP status of organizations and personnel.

Hazard Effects

In addition to threats, hazards can often have a significant effect on the Air Force and its mission in the form of major accidents and natural disasters. A major accident is

Disaster relief efforts, such as the response to Hurricane Katrina, are very visible examples of civil support in homeland operations.

an unplanned occurrence or the cumulative effect of a series of occurrences of such a magnitude as to warrant a significant response by the installation's disaster response force (DRF) and potentially community emergency response organizations. It differs from day-to-day emergencies and incidents that are routinely handled by base agencies without the DRF. A major accident may include unintentional incidents involving nuclear weapons, nuclear reactor facilities, hazardous materials (HAZMAT) spills, and aircraft crashes. Accidents have the potential to involve one or more of the following HAZMAT substances: radioactive materials, toxic industrial chemicals or materials, or explosives. The effects could include grave risk of injury or death to DOD or civilian personnel, extensive damage to public or private property, and adverse public reaction.

NATURAL DISASTERS AND FORCE PROTECTION

Like major accidents or terrorist incidents, natural disasters can also impact force protection and create emergency conditions that vary widely in scope, urgency, and degree of injury and destructive effects. Therefore, response, recovery, and mitigation actions will vary and may involve a national-level response. Natural disasters include earthquakes, extreme heat or cold, floods and flash floods, hurricanes or typhoons, landslides and mudflows, thunderstorms and lightning, tornadoes, extreme straight-line winds, cyclones, tsunamis, volcanoes, forest fires, avalanches, winter storms, and natural outbreaks of disease. Similar to major accidents, the effects could include mission degradation or stoppage, injury or death of DOD or civilian personnel, and extensive damage to public or private property.

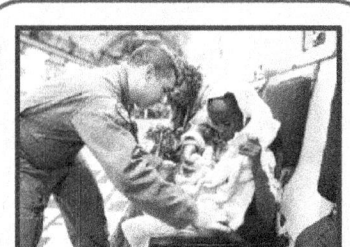

Staff Sergeant Timothy Valdez from the 4th Airlift Squadron, McChord AFB WA, helps a Haitian child. The Air Force responded to the 12 January 2010 earthquake that leveled much of the country's infrastructure.

Whether considering potential enemy or insider attacks, major accidents or natural disasters, an understanding of the threat objectives and hazard effects helps guide the planning to counter the threats and risks.

CHAPTER FOUR

FORCE PROTECTION PLANNING

> *If aircraft are vulnerable on the ground, why not attack them with every weapon available? That is just what the world's armies have done at least 645 times in ten conflicts between 1940 and 1992, destroying or damaging over 2,000 aircraft. ...[G]round attacks on airfields in past conflicts cannot be dismissed as a quaint subfield of military history. The basic techniques of airfield attack and defense have not changed dramatically over the past 50 years. The simple-but-effective tactics and the strategic rationale for the attacks are as relevant today as they were in 1940.*
>
> —**Alan Vick, *Snakes in the Eagle's Nest:***
> ***A History of Ground Attacks on Air Bases***

The essential goal of force protection is to counter threats and hazards against Air Force operations and assets. It is intended to conserve the force's fighting potential so it can be applied at the decisive time and place and incorporates the integrated and synchronized offensive and defensive measures to enable the effective employment of the force while degrading opportunities for the adversary.[29] Air Force personnel should identify threats and hazards, then determine ways to counter them to protect personnel and resources in order to enable mission accomplishment. This chapter identifies a set of FP tools for commanders to consider when preparing to counter threats and hazards. This begins with the risk management process and proceeds to FP countermeasure planning considerations.

RISK MANAGEMENT (RM) PROCESS

Commanders determine how best to manage risks. The Air Force defines risk management as **the process of identifying critical assets; understanding the threat; understanding Air Force vulnerabilities to the threat; determining risk to personnel, assets, and information; and assuming risk or applying countermeasures to correct or mitigate the risk.**[30] In all cases, the assessments include hazards as well as threats. This RM process consists of the following elements: prioritizing assets and resources by a **criticality assessment**, identifying potential threats through a **threat assessment**, analyzing resource and asset vulnerabilities through a **vulnerability assessment**, determining the risks acceptable to them for a given operation by conducting a **risk assessment**, then supervising and reviewing the effort to eliminate or mitigate the risks that are not acceptable. A safety and RM focus

---

[29] Information derived from JP 3-0, *Joint Operations*, page III-25, para 6.d.

[30] See AFI 31-101, *Integrated Defense*. This Air Force definition accords with and supports the joint definition of risk management: "The process of identifying, assessing, and controlling risks arising from operational factors and making decisions that balance risk cost with mission benefits." (JP 1-02)

ensures maximum protection of people and physical resources. This kind of risk-based focus is critical to warfighting success.

Safety, as applied via RM, is a major element of FP planning and should be used in the risk assessment phase of the RM process when planning to counter the threat or hazard. The operational risk management process established in Air Force safety channels, from identifying a hazard through implementing risk control measures and supervision and review of the effort, lends itself ideally to planning for FP efforts.[31] Safety has a strong impact on FP's overall effectiveness.[32] Figure 4.1 is an illustration of the RM process for FP.

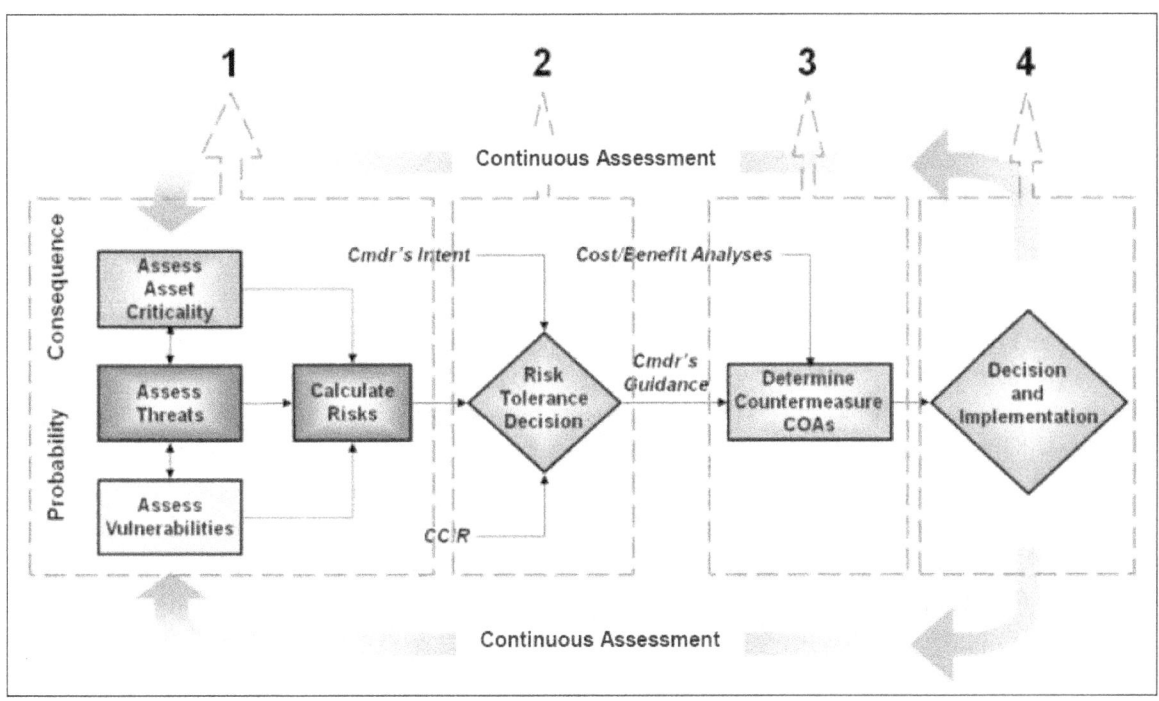

Figure 4.1. The Risk Management Process.
(Derived from AFI 31-101, *Integrated Defense*)

Criticality Assessment

A commander should know and identify those assets critical to mission execution. A criticality assessment is a systematic effort to identify key assets and infrastructure and evaluate the effect of temporary or permanent loss of the same on the installation's or a unit's ability to perform its mission. This assessment should examine costs of recovery and reconstitution including time, funds, capability, and infrastructure support. Assessments of non-mission essential assets should also be considered, such as high-population facilities; mass gathering activities; and other facilities, equipment, services, or resources deemed important by the commander to ensure continued

---

[31] See AFI 90-901, *Operational Risk Management.*
[32] See the 91-series of Air Force instructions for information on Air Force safety programs.

effective operation. This assessment also assists the commander in identifying assets that are priorities for FP resource allocation.

Assessing criticality requires judgment and analysis. For example, the destruction of an asset not considered essential to mission success or necessary for continued efficient operations may still be critical, if deemed symbolic by the enemy. Such an asset may warrant protection because its loss may give an enemy the media coverage they seek or cause personnel to doubt a commander's ability to keep them safe. Complete protection of every asset is not possible, but the more difficult it is for the enemy to act, the less likely he is to attack. The critical infrastructure program[33] is a complementary effort that seeks to identify, assess, and mitigate the vulnerabilities of the unit's most critical, single-point-failure assets, and should be used when identifying and assessing those assets critical to mission success.

Threat Assessment

A commander should know what threat or hazard is anticipated in order to devise an effective means to counter or mitigate it. Without this knowledge, the commander is acting blindly. A thorough threat assessment reviews the factors of a threat's or hazard's existence, capability, intention, history, and targeting, as well as the operating environment within which friendly forces operate. Analyzing and synthesizing this information are essential precursor steps in identifying the probability of attack or hazard event. AFOSI and other Service counterparts produce a defense threat assessment that should be used as a baseline product for adversarial threats in the FP effort. At the installation level, the threat working group or other intelligence fusion and analysis cell (e.g., joint intelligence support element, etc.) should assist in producing a localized threat assessment and recommend courses of action to the commander to mitigate or counter threats and hazards. Hazards should be evaluated for severity and frequency to determine how often they may affect an installation and the impact they may have to mission accomplishment.

In the complex environment of irregular warfare (IW), ISR forces should use information collected from a variety of sources to provide or collect information to fill intelligence gaps. ISR personnel should validate the credibility of these various sources to overcome adversary denial and deception, and information operations. Though rules of engagement and operational objectives drive operations, analysts should craft their intelligence requirements to account for both available kinetic and non-kinetic capabilities to prevent adverse effects on the population. Analysts should recognize an increased need to make correlations between various development projects and levels of cooperation with local nationals. Additionally, ISR forces should be aware that one of the basic underpinnings of successful IW operations is the capability to train partners to conduct independent operations and participate in coalition operations.

---

[33] For additional information on the critical infrastructure program, see Air Force Policy Directive (AFPD) 10-24, *Critical Infrastructure Program.* This supports Homeland Security Presidential Directive 7, *Critical Infrastructure Identification, Prioritization, and Protection*, and DODD 3020.40, *DOD Policy and Responsibilities for Critical Infrastructure.*

Threat assessments fuse information and intelligence from open source, law enforcement, government intelligence, and counterintelligence information, along with local, state, and federal information to create a cohesive threat picture for FP decision-makers. By synthesizing law enforcement, intelligence, and counterintelligence information, analysts can identify indicators of future attacks. The more common sources are described in Figure 4.2.[34]

OPEN SOURCE INFORMATION: 　—News media, hearings, publications, reference services, private data services, internet
LAW ENFORCEMENT INFORMATION: 　—Collection, retention, and dissemination regulated by law enforcement channels 　—Law enforcement information
GOVERNMENT INTELLIGENCE AND COUNTERINTELLIGENCE INFORMATION: 　—Products and reporting from the US intelligence community
LOCAL, STATE, AND FEDERAL INFORMATION (including host nation): 　—Service member, civil servant, family member, individuals with regional knowledge 　—Counterintelligence force protection operations—information gleaned from the streets

Figure 4.2. Sources of Intelligence and Counterintelligence.

Considering the wide range of possible threats and hazards, FP personnel should focus on developing a robust FPI threat picture to support unit deployments, readiness training, mission planning, and other mission execution functions such as integrated defense, the critical infrastructure program, and emergency management.[35] Commanders should develop priority intelligence requirements to guide FPI work supporting their decision-making and operations. FP personnel should coordinate with their cross-functional counterparts to ensure information requirements are satisfied. Once FP information has been fused, the end product should be provided to the commander to guide intelligence-driven and risk-based measures or operations, such as counterthreat operations, to preempt, deter, mitigate, or negate threats and hazards. FPI provides support to all phases of FP operations.[36]

---

[34] See JP 3-07.2, *Antiterrorism*.
[35] See AFTTP 3-10.1, *Integrated Base Defense*; AFPD 10-24, *Air Force Critical Infrastructure Program (CIP)*; and AFI 10-2501, *Air Force Emergency Management (EM) Program Planning and Operations*, for more information on these functions.
[36] For additional information, see AFI 14-119, *Intelligence Support to Force Protection (FP)*.

Vulnerability Assessment

Once the threat assessment is complete, commanders should prepare a vulnerability assessment of their personnel, equipment, facilities, installations, and operating areas. This assessment should address the broad range of physical threats to the security of the commander's personnel and assets. The vulnerability assessment then considers the identified and projected threats against personnel, facilities, or other assets to identify those areas where resources are susceptible to actions which may reduce or diminish operational effectiveness. This includes the local populace and infrastructure due to association or proximity with Air Force operations.

Airmen should consider both the threat and existing vulnerabilities, but should not rely exclusively on the assessed threat. For example, terrorists successfully attacked military targets, such as Khobar Towers, the USS Cole, and three residential compounds in Riyadh, Saudi Arabia, even though those locations were in FPCON Bravo. Non-military targets, such as the US embassies in Tanzania and Kenya or the World Trade Center, have been attacked when the country terrorist threat assessments for those locations were moderate, low, or negligible.[37] History shows that the assessed threat is not necessarily an accurate reflection of the actual threat. As a result, identifying vulnerabilities is critical. Once identified, steps to mitigate the vulnerabilities should be undertaken to increase survivability for Air Force personnel and assets.

Risk Assessment

Finally, upon completion of the criticality, threat, and vulnerability assessments, commanders should have the information they need to make decisions regarding what level of risk they are willing to accept. Ultimately commanders decide what level of risk to accept. However, risks to the most critical Air Force assets should be mitigated or eliminated whenever possible. If risks cannot be eliminated, commanders should implement measures to mitigate them to the greatest extent possible. An example of the risk assessment process is provided in Figure 4.3.

---

[37] Information derived from AFDD 2-4.1, *Force Protection*, 9 Nov 04.

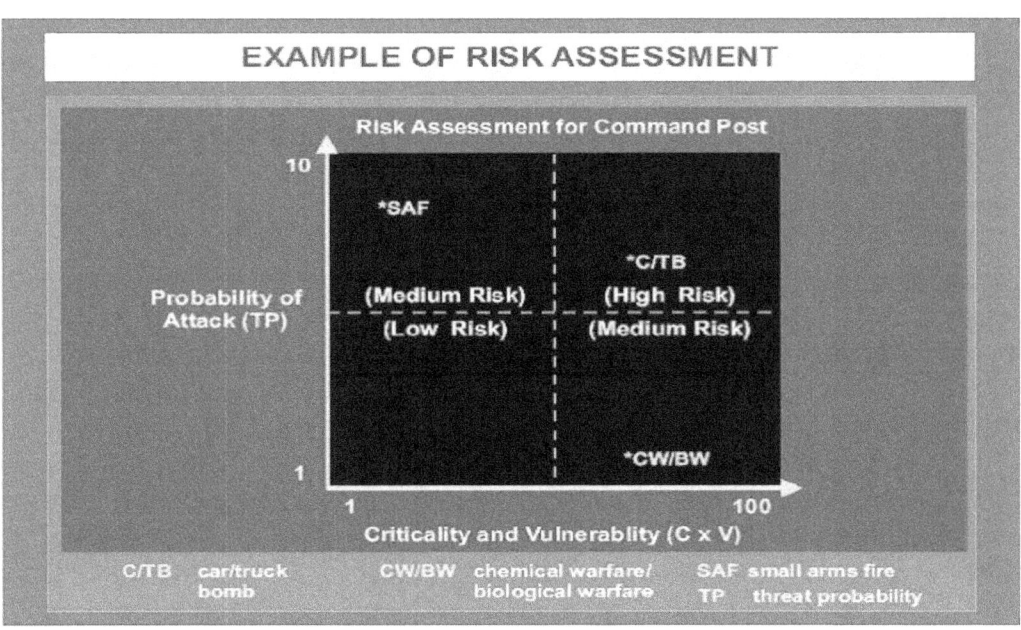

Figure 4.3. Example of Risk Assessment

FORCE PROTECTION PLANNING

Because threats and hazards to operations can come from a wide range of sources, the Airman's perspective requires Airmen to plan for FP in broader terms than other surface-oriented organizations. For example, the threats to an active airfield may extend far beyond the surface area designated as a base boundary. To address these threats, the Air Force uses the planning construct of the BSZ to ensure those ground threats and hazards that could impact operations are considered and planned for.

Base Security Zone

The multi-dimensional space around the base from which the enemy might impact air operations by launching an attack against approaching or departing aircraft or personnel and resources located on the base is critical to air base defense planning. To secure airpower and protect personnel and resources in this area, the Air Force uses a unique planning construct, referred to as the BSZ.[38] Focused intelligence preparation of the operating environment (IPOE) efforts and integrated defense operations should operate in unison to support BSZ establishment. Security planners

Airmen from the 532nd Expeditionary Security Forces Squadron search a field during a force protection patrol outside Joint Base Balad, Iraq, 17 October 2009.

---

[38] See AFPD 31-1, *Integrated Defense*, for information that establishes the BSZ as an Air Force construct.

should first establish this planning construct through IPOE and commander's estimate, and then seek to align it with the negotiated base boundary—the area allocated to the base commander for protection. Should the derived area extend beyond the base boundary into the BSZ, and alignment with the base boundary is not possible, then Air Force security planners should coordinate with battlespace owners to ensure the protection of airpower resources.

Base Boundary

JP 3-10, *Joint Security Operations in Theater*, identifies the base boundary as a line that delineates the surface area of a base for the purpose of facilitating coordination and deconfliction of operations between adjacent units, formations, or areas. The base boundary, which is not necessarily the base perimeter, is negotiated on a case-by-case basis between the base commander and the area commander or host-nation authority. The base boundary should be established based upon the factors of mission, enemy, terrain and weather, troops and support available, time available, and civil considerations, specifically balancing the need of the base defense forces to control key terrain with their ability to accomplish the mission. Whenever an Air Force commander is designated the base commander of a joint use base, he or she should use the base boundary construct in establishing base defense plans as it most readily translates to effective plans for the other Services present on the base. If the base boundary does not include all of the terrain of concern to the senior Air Force commander (if not the base commander), as identified by the BSZ, he or she should advise the base commander of the responsibility to either mitigate (through coordination with the area commander or the

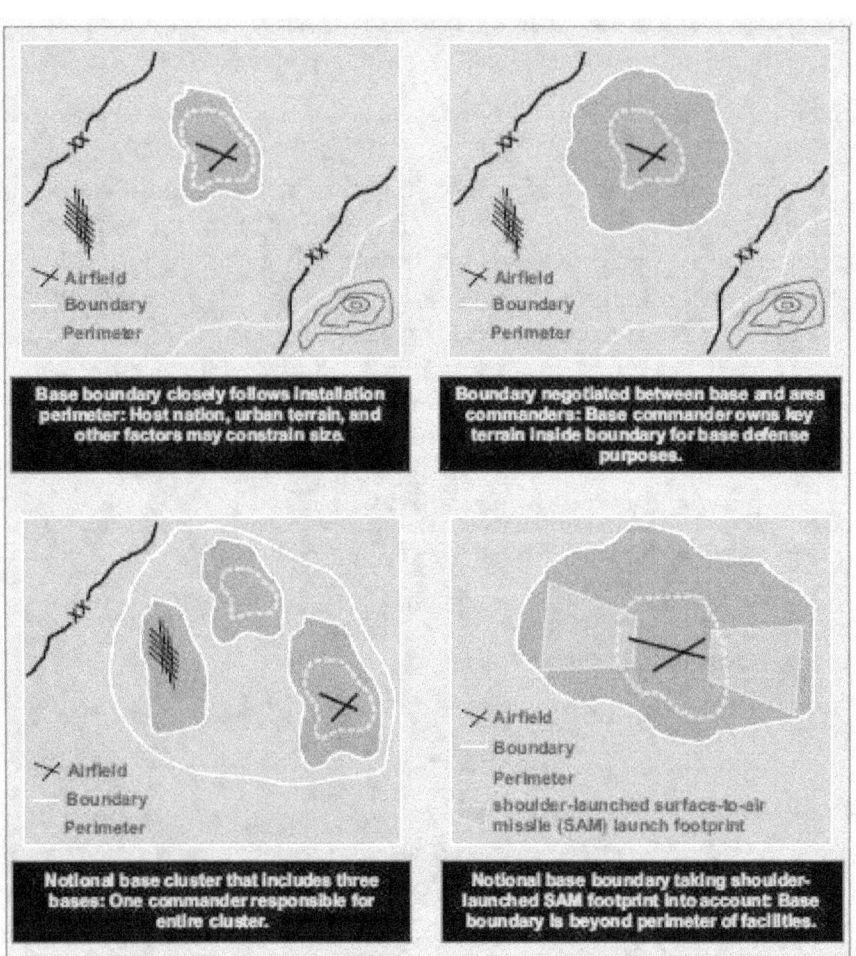

Figure 4.4. Base Boundary considerations.
Information from JP 3-10, *Joint Security Operations in Theater*.

28

host nation) or accept the risks of enemy attack from the area outside the base boundary. Figure 4.4 illustrates base boundary considerations.

FORCE PROTECTION INTELLIGENCE

Airmen are subject to threats whether in the CONUS or outside the CONUS (OCONUS). These threats and hazards are continually evolving and will increasingly challenge US personnel, facilities, and assets. Understanding how these threat and hazard elements function is the first step to developing an effective FP program that will help commanders assess their ability to respond to an incident.

As such, tailored FPI is fundamental to the prosecution of an effective FP program. It is a mission set used to identify intelligence support to FP. All-source intelligence should be provided on threats or hazards to DOD missions, people or resources stemming from terrorists, criminal entities, FISS, and opposing military forces as appropriate under Presidential executive order 12333. [39]

Intelligence is a major enabler that supports FP decisions and operations. It is a collaborative effort between intelligence, counterintelligence, and Security Forces. However, the roles of each differ depending on location (CONUS/OCONUS) due to executive orders and other policies. The end result of this vital function is a more accurate picture for commanders at all organizational levels, enhancing the protection of personnel, resources, and information. Figure 4.5 illustrates the collaborative nature of FPI among the key performers of FPI efforts.

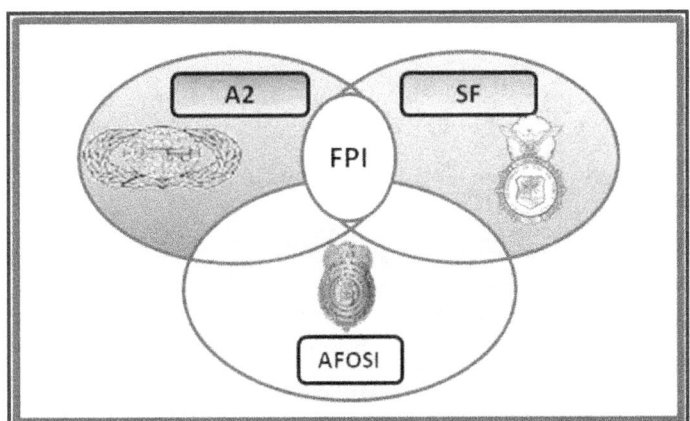

Figure 4.5. Force Protection Intelligence Construct

---

[39] FPI deals specifically with intelligence efforts to counter enemy threats. Those intelligence efforts that address hazards are referred to as incident awareness and assessment. For additional information on incident awareness and assessment, see AFDD 2-0, *Global Integrated Intelligence, Surveillance, and Reconnaissance.*

COUNTERTHREAT OPERATIONS (CTO)

Counterthreat operations are defined as the employment of AFOSI capabilities to find, fix, track, and neutralize enemy threats in order to create a sustained permissive environment for air, space, and cyberspace operations.[40] CTO are essential in detecting, assessing, denying, and responding to threats affecting Air Force operations. CTO are ISR-driven operations using information derived from multiple intelligence and counterintelligence sources providing tactical situational awareness to forewarn or preempt enemy or adversarial attack. CTO activities include counterintelligence collection, analysis, and investigation; surveillance; and countersurveillance. These activities provide excellent sources of intelligence that assist FP operations. The base defense forces should use ISR to aggressively eliminate threats. The ability to acquire and analyze suspicious activity reports for indications and warning of possible terrorist pre-attack activities is a critical component of counterintelligence support to the force protection mission. Terrorists have the advantage of choosing the time and venue for their attacks, but normally have to conduct extensive pre-attack preparations to maximize their chances of success. The pre-attack phase of a terrorist operation, however, is the period of greatest vulnerability to the terrorist group, since it must surface to collect intelligence and conduct physical surveillance and other activities of the target. Therefore, an effective system, such as CTO, for detecting terrorist pre-attack activities is a high priority task for the intelligence community, law enforcement, security elements, and local community authorities.

A tactical security element of AFOSI and Security Forces personnel confirms grid coordinates it investigated during a search and capture mission, 30 March 2010, in Parwan Province, Afghanistan.

---

[40] See AFTTP 3-10.3, *Integrated Base Defense Counterthreat Operations*, for more information on CTO.

CHAPTER FIVE

THE FORCE PROTECTION COMMUNITY

> *Every airman should have his place in the defence scheme…. Every airfield should be a stronghold of fighting air-groundsmen, and not the abode of uniformed civilians in the prime of life protected by detachments of soldiers.*
>
> **—Sir Winston Churchill,**
> **29 June 1941 memo to the Secretary of State for Air and Chief of Air Staff**

Force protection is achieved through the successful execution of three related but distinct lines of effort: integrated defense, emergency management, and the critical infrastructure program. These lines of effort are supported by programs and activities contributing to FP through integration of multifunctional capabilities and activities. The purpose is to integrate these capabilities to achieve the desired FP effects of detect, deter, preempt, negate, and mitigate. Integration of all the programs and activities is the means to achieve successful FP.

INTEGRATED DEFENSE

Effective integrated defense helps ensure effective FP. While integrated defense is an Air Force-wide responsibility, Air Force Security Forces are the Service enterprise lead for integrated defense operations, synchronizing Air Force policy pertaining to protection and defense against all threats and hazards to Air Force installations. The defense force commander (DFC) employs Air Force Security Forces and other multidisciplinary resources and personnel to execute this operation. The DFC integrates operations with emergency management activities. Integrated defense operations protect and defend Air Force personnel, installations, activities, infrastructure, resources, and information. Integrated defense requires timely FPI. Commanders should use FPI to support decision-making for operations. Integrated defense relies on the ability of all Airmen to contribute to the defense of their installation while still fulfilling their primary functions.

Integrated defense is conducted worldwide, from mature theaters to austere regions. Air Force leadership should adapt to a variety of operational requirements. Some Air Force resources may be geographically separated from the main base. For example, communications facilities are often isolated and sited on high ground to maximize their effectiveness. Regardless of location, forces conducting integrated defense employ the basic tactics, techniques, and procedures as those employed at home station during day-to-day operations. As specific threats to base personnel and resources increase, integrated defense forces adjust tactics to counter the threat. Adjustments to operating procedures should be based on the specific threat to operations, the dynamics of operating in an international environment or the way integrated defense efforts collaborate with joint, combined, civilian, and host nation forces. Integrated defense forces should be prepared to operate at a variety of locations and may deploy to sites without existing Air Force or host nation facilities.

EMERGENCY MANAGEMENT

The protection of Air Force personnel and resources on Air Force installations is essential to ensure successful Air Force operations. The Air Force Emergency Management Program addresses activities across the all-hazards physical threat environment at CONUS and OCONUS home station or expeditionary locations to support overall FP. Figure 5.1 illustrates the Air Force's emergency management construct.

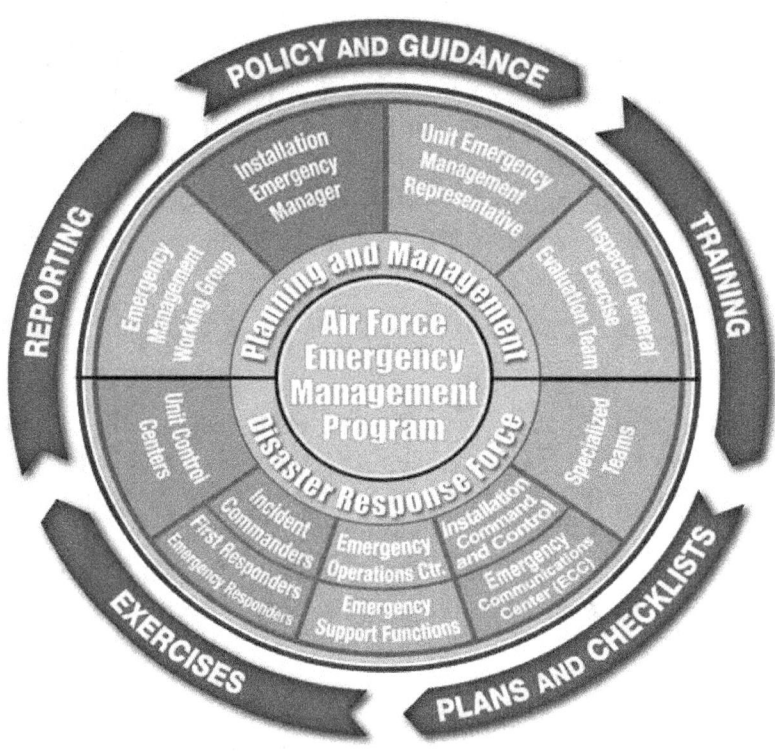

Figure 5.1. The Air Force Emergency Management Program Construct

The primary mission focus of emergency management (EM) is to save lives; minimize the loss or degradation of resources; and continue, sustain, and restore operational capability in an all-hazards physical threat environment at Air Force installations worldwide. These physical threats may occur at any time, with or without prior warning. Emergency management supports protection of personnel and resources through integration of installation preparedness, response, and recovery programs aimed toward reducing the impact of these events on the installation; prepares for risks that cannot be eliminated; and prescribes actions required to deal with consequences of actual events and to recover from those events using the Air Force Incident Management System (AFIMS). Emergency management planning and response is based on National Incident Management System methodology to align with the National Response Framework as directed by Homeland Security Presidential Directive 5. See AFPD 10-25, *Emergency Management,* and DOD 6055-17, *DOD Installation Emergency Management (IEM) Program*, for more information on the installation emergency management program.

CRITICAL INFRASTRUCTURE PROGRAM

Operations in support of the National Military Strategy are dependent on globally linked physical and cyber infrastructures (US and foreign, public and private sector). These interconnected infrastructures, while improving capabilities and mission effectiveness, also increase vulnerability to potential failures due to human error, natural disasters, or intentional attack. Consequently, it is important to identify and protect those infrastructures critical to mission accomplishment.

FORCE PROTECTION EFFECTS

Threats to Air Force interests occur across the ROMO from peacetime through wartime. Commanders should recognize that any given threat may be present at any time. Commanders should also consider the effects intended to be produced by the threat, not just the nature of the threat itself. In this manner, a threat can be small in execution with large-scale effects as the outcome; threats can undermine mission capability as severely as sabotage or engagement with enemy forces. FP efforts conserve the Air Force's fighting potential by safeguarding its forces and mission capability through the achievement of predetermined effects. In all circumstances, commanders should tailor resources and capabilities to achieve, at minimum, the following FP effects:

☼ Deter—Measures should be developed to discourage adversarial actions. Vital to the effectiveness of these measures is the existence of a credible threat of unacceptable counteraction. Potential adversaries should perceive the Air Force has the capability to conduct and sustain offensive and defensive operations. This is best achieved through the possession of forces properly trained, organized, and equipped to execute base security against unconventional, Level I and II threats, and, if required, engage Level III threats and conduct a combat handover to a tactical combat force.

☼ Detect—Measures should be developed to identify the presence of an object or an event of possible military interest, whether a threat or hazard. Detection may arise through observation of the operational area or through deductions made following an analysis of the operational area.

☼ Preempt—Once conclusive evidence indicating an imminent enemy attack is determined, actions should be initiated to rapidly respond and establish or gain a position of advantage to eliminate the threat. Essential to effective preemptive operations is an accurate estimate of the adversary's capabilities and vulnerabilities.

Every intelligence and counterintelligence resource available should be used to determine enemy capabilities, intentions, and probable courses of action.

○ Negate—Measures should be taken to render a threat or hazard incapable of interfering with Air Force operations. This includes the effective employment of coordinated and synchronized offensive and defensive measures and measures to counteract hazards.

○ Mitigate—If actions to negate are unsuccessful, measures should be taken to minimize enemy success and lessen the consequence or severity of the adversary's actions. Likewise, measures should be taken to reduce the consequences of any hazard affecting operations.

CONCLUSION

While the bombing of the Marine barracks in Lebanon in October 1983 marked the beginning of terrorist attacks by violent Islamic extremists upon the US military, it was not until their attack upon Khobar Towers in 1996 that protecting the force against a terrorist enemy rose to a more prominent role in military operations. Since the Khobar Towers attack, the trend of terror attacks has grown in frequency and lethality. The current level of threats to Air Force people and resources dictates that the Service take strong measures to protect its forces at home and when deployed. Protecting Air Force personnel and resources is critical to its ability to perform its missions. Air Force forces are poised to respond to global taskings at any time; force protection enables this capability.

The Air Force's holistic approach to FP permits the Service to address threats and hazards to its personnel and resources from all sources, natural or manmade. The changing methods of attack used by adversaries require the Air Force to consider the nontraditional ways in which it may be attacked and how to counter these elusive threats. Airmen must be increasingly vigilant, using all the various expertise available to counter threats to Air Force operations and hazards to Air Force personnel and resources.

Because FP responsibility flows from combatant commanders, this responsibility permeates all levels of command, which then reaches to all Airmen, everywhere. Commanders at all levels should aggressively execute their force protection responsibilities and programs. Commanders are responsible for protecting their people and the resources used to perform military operations.

Every Airman is responsible for the execution of appropriate FP measures, which ensures the greatest opportunity to protect the force as a whole. Airmen are obligated by the moral necessity of protecting our fellow Airmen to ensure force protection is a part of Air Force culture.

AT THE VERY HEART OF WARFARE LIES DOCTRINE....

SUGGESTED READINGS

All Air Force personnel should be familiar with the full breadth of Air Force operations. As a beginning, they should read the entire series of the basic and operational doctrine documents. Air Force doctrine documents are available online at: https://wwwmil.maxwell.af.mil/au/lemay/main.asp
or the LeMay Center for Doctrine Development and Education's Community of Practice website:
https://afkm.wpafb.af.mil/ASPs/CoP/OpenCoP.asp?Filter=OO-OP-AF-44.

AIR FORCE PUBLICATIONS

AFI 10-208, *Continuity of Operations Program (COOP)*
AFI 10-245, *Antiterrorism (AT)*
AFI 10-2501, *Air Force Emergency Management (EM) Program Planning and Operations*
AFI 10-2603, *Emergency Health Powers on Air Force Installations*
AFI 10-2604, *Disease Containment Planning*
AFI 14-104, *Oversight of Intelligence Activities*
AFI 14-119, *Intelligence Support to Force Protection (FP)*
AFI 31-101, *Integrated Defense (FOUO)*
AFI 90-901, *Operational Risk Management*

AFPD 10-8, *Homeland Defense and Civil Support*
AFPD 10-24, *Air Force Critical Infrastructure Program*
AFPD 10-25, *Emergency Management*
AFPD 10-26, *Counter-Chemical, Biological, Radiological, and Nuclear Operations*
AFPD 31-1, *Integrated Defense*
AFPD 90-9, *Operational Risk Management*

Air Force Pamphlet (AFP) 10-100, *Airman's Manual*
AFP 90-902, *Operational Risk Management (ORM) Guidelines and Tools*

Air Force Tactics, Techniques, and Procedures (AFTTP) 3-2.42, *Multi-Service Tactics, Techniques, and Procedures for Nuclear, Biological, and Chemical Defense Operations*
AFTTP 3-2.46, *Multi-Service Tactics, Techniques, and Procedures for Nuclear, Biological, and Chemical Defense Operations*
AFTTP 3-10.1, *Integrated Base Defense (IBD)*
AFTTP 3-10.2, *Integrated Base Defense Command and Control*
AFTTP 3-10.3, *Integrated Defense Counter Threat Operations (CTO)*

JOINT PUBLICATIONS

JP 1, *Doctrine for the Armed Forces of the United States*
JP 1-02, *Department of Defense Dictionary of Military and Associated Terms*

JP 3-0, *Joint Operations*
JP 3-01, *Countering Air and Missile Threats*
JP 3-07.2, *Antiterrorism*
JP 3-10, *Joint Security Operations in Theater*
JP 3-11, *Operations in Chemical, Biological, Radiological, and Nuclear (CBRN) Environments*
JP 3-13, *Information Operations*
JP 3-40, *Combating Weapons of Mass Destruction*

DOD Directive 2000.12, *DOD Antiterrorism (AT) Program*
DOD Directive 3020.40, *DOD Policy and Responsibilities for Critical Infrastructure*
DOD Directive 5200.27, *Acquisition of Information Concerning Persons and Organizations Not Affiliated with the Department of Defense*
DOD Regulation 5240.1-R, *Procedures Governing the Activities of DOD Intelligence Components That Affect US Persons*
DOD Instruction 2000.16, *DOD Antiterrorism (AT) Standards*
DOD Instruction 5200.08, *Security of DOD Installations and Resources and the DOD Physical Security Review Board (PSRB)*
DOD 5200.08-R, *Physical Security Program*
DOD O-2000.12-H, *DOD Antiterrorism Handbook*
DOD 4500.54-G, *Department of Defense Foreign Clearance Guide*

Memorandum of Understanding Between the Department of State and DOD on Security of DOD Elements and Personnel in Foreign Areas

OTHER PUBLICATIONS

Department of State, *Patterns of Global Terrorism*
Fox, Roger P., *Air Base Defense in the Republic of Vietnam: 1961-1973*, (USAF Office of History), 1979.
Grant, Rebecca, *Khobar Towers,* AIR FORCE Magazine, June 1998, Vol. 81, No. 6.
Nolan, Keith William, *The Battle for Saigon—Tet 1968*, (Pocket Books), 1996.
Shlapak, David A. and Alan Vick, *Check Six Begins on the Ground*, (RAND), 1995.
Vick, Alan, *Snakes in the Eagle's Nest*, (RAND), 1995.
Joint Airfield/Airbase Initial Impressions Report, July 2005.
Fighting Air Bases Under Attack: Forward Operating Bases (draft), RAND Corporation Study, 2005.
HQ ACC/SF Force Protection Study (Iraq Trip Report), Col Mary Kay Hertog, December 2003.

GLOSSARY

ABBREVIATIONS AND ACRONYMS

ADCON	administrative control
AFDD	Air Force doctrine document
AFI	Air Force instruction
AFOSI	Air Force Office of Special Investigations
AFPD	Air Force policy directive
AFTTP	Air Force tactics, techniques, and procedures
AOR	area of responsibility
AT	antiterrorism
BSZ	base security zone
CBRN	chemical, biological, radiological, and nuclear
CBRNE	chemical, biological, radiological, nuclear, and high-yield explosives
COMAFFOR	commander, Air Force forces
CONUS	continental United States
CTO	counterthreat operations
DFC	defense force commander
DIA	Defense Intelligence Agency
DOD	Department of Defense
DRF	disaster response force
FISS	foreign intelligence and security service
FP	force protection
FPCON	force protection condition
FPI	force protection intelligence
GCC	geographic combatant commander
HAZMAT	hazardous materials
IED	improvised explosive device
IPOE	intelligence preparation of the operational environment
ISR	intelligence, surveillance, and reconnaissance
IW	irregular warfare
JFC	joint force commander
JP	joint publication
JTF	joint task force

NATO	North Atlantic Treaty Organization
OCONUS	outside the continental United States
OPCON	operational control
OPM-SANG	Office of Program Manager-Saudi Arabian National Guard
RM	risk management
ROMO	range of military operations
SAM	surface-to-air-missile
TACON	tactical control
USNORTHCOM	United States Northern Command
VBIED	vehicle-borne improvised explosive device
WMD	weapon of mass destruction

DEFINITIONS

antiterrorism. Defensive measures used to reduce the vulnerability of individuals and property to terrorist acts, to include rapid containment by local military and civilian forces. Also called **AT**. (JP 1-02)

base commander. In base defense operations, the officer assigned to command a base. (JP 1-02)

base boundary. A line that delineates the surface area of a base for the purpose of facilitating coordination and deconfliction of operation between adjacent units, formations, or areas. (JP 1-02)

base security zone. The battlespace from which the enemy can launch an attack against base personnel and resources or aircraft approaching/departing the base. Also called **BSZ**. (AFTTP 3-10.2)

combating terrorism. Actions, including antiterrorism and counterterrorism, taken to oppose terrorism throughout the entire threat spectrum. Also called **CbT**. (JP 1-02)

countermeasures. That form of military science that, by the employment of devices and/or techniques, has as its objective the impairment of the operational effectiveness of enemy activity. (JP 1-02)

counterthreat operations. The AFOSI's capability to find, fix, track, and neutralize enemy threats in order to create a sustained permissive environment for air, space, and cyberspace operations.   Also called **CTO**. (AFDD 3-10)

defense force commander. The senior Air Force commander responsible for the air base normally delegates operational authority to conduct integrated base defense to the defense force commander. The defense force commander exercises command and control through an established chain of command and directs the planning and execution of base defense operations. Also called **DFC**. (AFTTP 3-10.1)

force health protection. Measures to promote, improve, or conserve the mental and physical well-being of Service members. These measures enable a healthy and fit force, prevent injury and illness, and protect the force from health hazards. Also called **FHP**. (JP 1-02) [*A comprehensive threat-based program directed at preventing and managing health-related actions against Air Force uncommitted combat power.*] (AFDD 4-02) {Italicized definition in brackets applies only to the Air Force and is offered for clarity.}

force protection. Preventive measures taken to mitigate hostile actions against Department of Defense personnel (to include family members), resources, facilities, and critical information. Force protection does not include actions to defeat the enemy or protect against accidents, weather, or disease. Also called **FP**. (JP 1-02) [*The process of detecting threats and hazards to the Air Force and its mission, and applying measures to deter, pre-empt, negate or mitigate them based on an acceptable level of risk.*] (AFDD 3-10) {Italicized definition in brackets applies only to the Air Force and is offered for clarity.}

force protection intelligence. Analyzed, all-source information concerning threats to DOD missions, people, or resources arising from terrorists, criminal entities, foreign intelligence and security services and opposing military forces. Also called **FPI**. (AFTTP 3-10.2)

integrated defense. The integration of multidisciplinary active and passive, offensive and defensive capabilities, employed to mitigate potential risks and defeat adversary threats to Air Force operations. (AFI 31-101)

intelligence fusion cell. Cell providing the base defense force with analyzed or vetted all-source information that drives effective force protection decisions and operations. (AFTTP 3-10.2).